BIRCH
BOOKS

First published by Birch Books 2020

ISBN (978-81-949495-4-1)

Email : books.birch@gmail.com

SHERA AND HIRA IN THREE QUESTIONS

RUCHIRA DARDA

For Aryaveer and Adhiraj.
For teaching me a new
lesson in parenting each day.

Dear Parent,

As a young mother, getting parenthood right was my only mission. I yearned for someone to tell me what is it that I must do. One day I stumbled upon the idea of The Three Questions.

It told me everything I needed to know. It allowed my kids to be vulnerable and share their joys and their sorrows.

After a couple of years of following this routine at bedtime we stopped doing it as a practice, but when my children wanted to share something with me and didn't know how to begin the conversation they began to use this technique. For me this was magical, for a child to use a skill to express and begin discussions and sharing.

Hence, I present to you the gift of these questions. Remember to keep your sharing honest.

Happy Parenting!

Love

Ruchira Darda

"I won't go to school anymore."
He grunted.

"Why not, my darling?"
Hira asked lovingly.

She had put the meal aside and stopped to listen to her cub. As she moved forward to kiss him, Shera pushed back and asserted, "No, I won't go to school."

"Alright, don't go from tomorrow.
Freshen up, lunch is almost ready."

That evening,
Hira waited for Shera to return home from the nearby lake,
where he was swimming with his friends.

Shera pounced on Hira excitedly.
He shared stories of how they had managed to cross the lake without getting wet and then playfully splashed water on everyone crossing by.
Hira allowed Shera to revel in each moment.

At bedtime,
while the young cub still
continued with his tales of
the evening that had gone by,
Hira slipped in a question,

"What was the best part of
your day?"

"The lake", Shera was quick to answer.

"What was the worst part of your day?"

Shera looked away.
Hira said, "The best part of my day was that I was able to finish the puzzle I started."

She continued,
"The worst part of my day was that I got a scolding from my art teacher for not having finished the task he had given me on time."

"But I assured him I will do it promptly tomorrow so he wasn't angry anymore."

As Shera heard his mother's story of failure,
he gathered courage to share his own.
"Today in school,
Mr Boar, the guard, angrily
held me in front of everyone.
That was my worst thing.
I will never go to school again."

"Oh really? That's not nice of Mr Boar...
but why did he do that?
Did you do something he didn't approve of?"

"No, I didn't"

"Hmm, I don't understand why he would punish you...
I am going to go and have a word with him
and maybe complain to the Principal, my poor baby."

Hira looked to the side hoping
Shera would share more.

But he remained silent.

Hira asked her a third question,
"Tell me a secret?"

"My secret,
remember you can't share this with anyone.
When your father left for a hunt this morning,
I managed to wrap and hide his
birthday present for him to discover tomorrow.
I am sure he will be pleasantly surprised."

"All the kids in the herd that go to
school together were calling
Mr Boar mean names,
so did I. All the other animal cubs ran away,
he caught me and scolded me.
I will never go back to school.
He might punish me more."

"Don't worry, he won't.
Tomorrow I will come with you to
the herd and we will both apologise to him."

"He might attack us!!!"

"He won't, don't worry. I am with you.
But next time, don't tease anyone, it hurts.
I would have also been upset
if someone called me by different names."

The next day,
Shera hid between his mother's paws as
they approached Mr Boar.
The gentle Mr Boar waved to Shera.
He had forgotten all about the previous day.
Shera murmured a sorry.
The kind Mr Boar lowered his paw and
rustled Shera's mane.
Shera realised in that moment that
he had always been extremely fond of Mr Boar.
It was Mr Boar who had held him when
he was a crying cub during playschool years, right
until his mother would come to pick him up.
He embraced Mr Boar and chimed another apology.
They went on to exchange a paw pat.

Shera turned around and ran back to Hira. He whispered a thank you in his mother's ears before he joined his friends at school.

Why don't you try asking these 3 questions:

1. What was the best part of your day?

2. What was the worst part of today?

3. Tell me a secret.

ABOUT THE AUTHOR

Ruchira Darda is a parent to two inspiring young children. They spend time together weaving stories and exploring the world through them.

Ruchira has a decade of experience working with children via her children's enrichment centre - The Yellow Door. Her pursuit of spirituality is the purpose behind her storytelling. She is an expert on personalities and is a sought after Relationship and Parenting Coach.
Her quest for spirituality coupled with her experience with women and children has led her to simplifying her learnings for children.

While she believes spiritual learning should come to children from a young age she also believes that everything we say to our children doesn't need to be so structured. That's why her storytelling is a blend of spurts of laughter, tamed with a dose of goodness.